.25

BOOK 5

Grand Trios For Piano

4 Intermediate Pieces for One Piano, Six Hands

Melody Bober

Trio playing is both energizing and exciting, and there are many ensemble possibilities: a teacher and two students; a parent and two siblings; or, my favorite, three friends. While performances can be thrilling, preparing trio music can be enjoyable as well since sharing the love of music with others is so rewarding.

Trios also offer a great musical experience for students. Rhythm, phrasing, articulation, and dynamics all become wonderful teaching tools while students learn to listen for that unique blending of parts. I have written *Grand Trios for Piano*, Book 5, so that today's piano students can experience music in a variety of styles, meters, and tempos. I have also written this collection so that students can progress technically and musically...together!

I sincerely hope that students will find the pieces challenging and fun in these *Grand Trios for Piano*!

Best wishes,

CONTENTS

A Chilly Nor'easter 2

Chromatic Waltz. 8

El Matador 16

Riverbend Rag 24

A solo version of "El Matador" is available in *Grand Solos for Piano,* book 4 (#30112).

Alfred Music Publishing Co., Inc.
P.O. Box 10003
Van Nuys, CA 91410-0003
alfred.com

ISBN-10: 0-7390-9364-9
ISBN-13: 978-0-7390-9364-1

Cover Photos
stage lights: © stock.xchng/photos71

A Chilly Nor'easter

Melody Bober

Middle

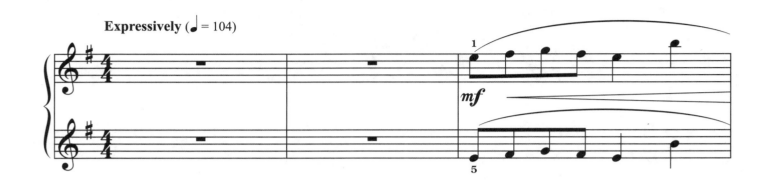

Low

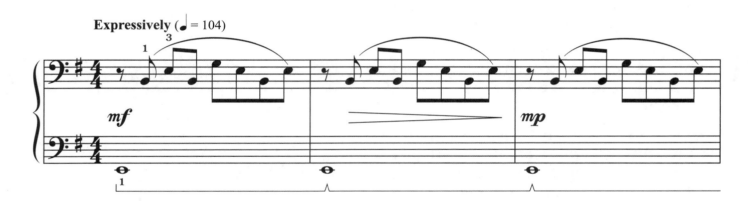

Middle

Low . . . .

High

Middle

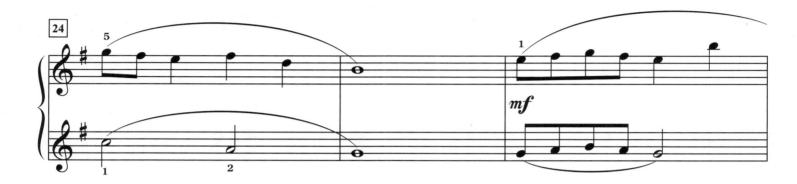

Low

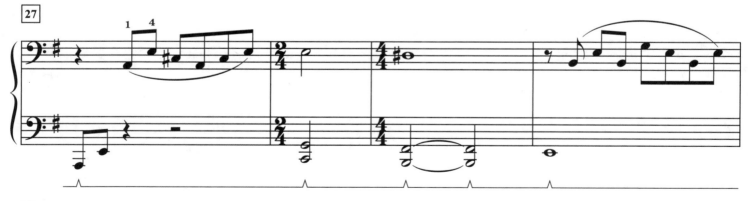

High

Chromatic Waltz

Melody Bober

Middle

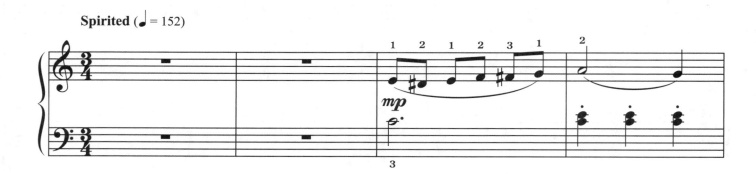

Low

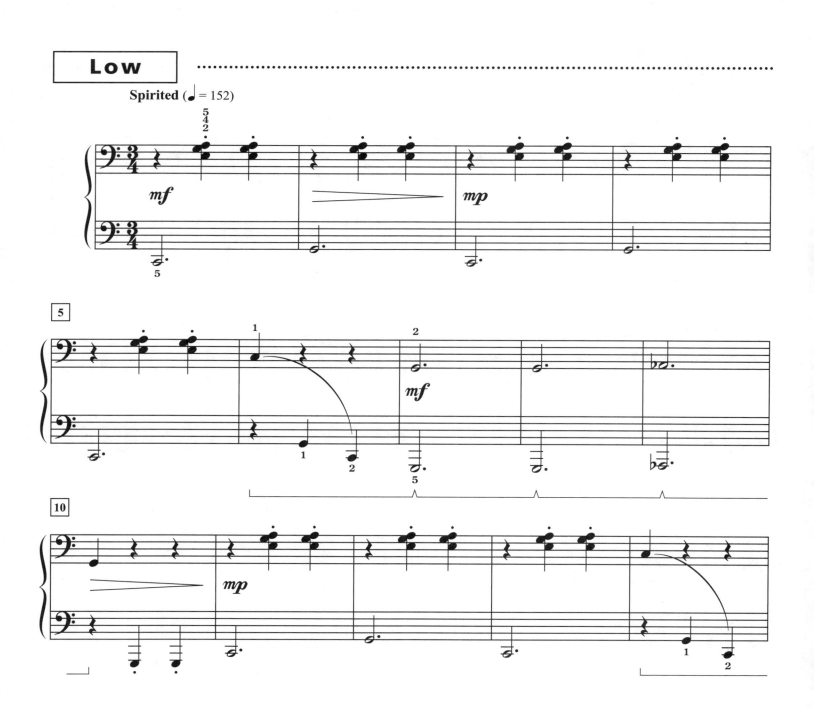

High

Both hands one octave higher throughout

Spirited (♩ = 152)

Middle

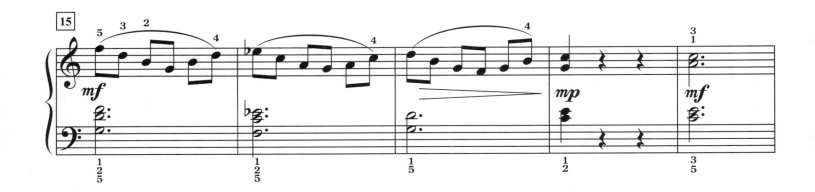

Low

Middle

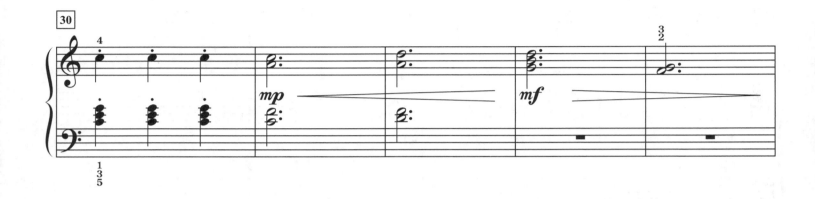

Low

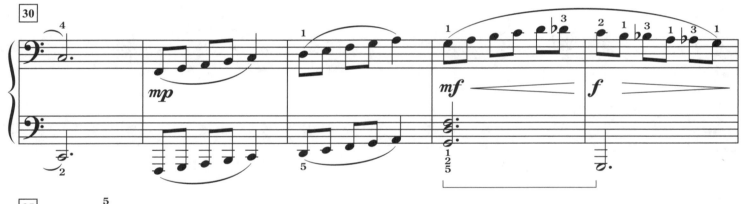

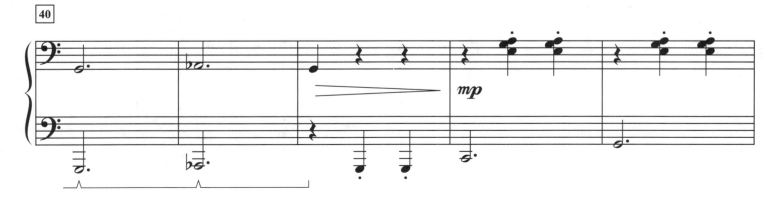

Middle

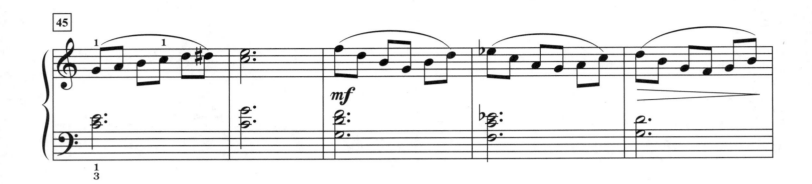

Low

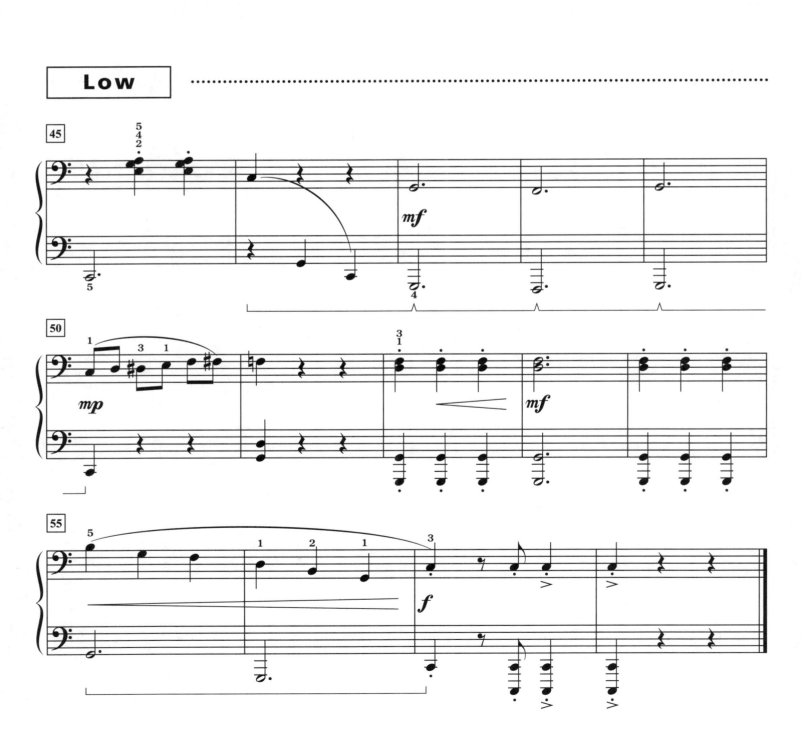

El Matador

Melody Bober

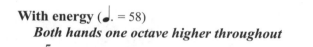

High

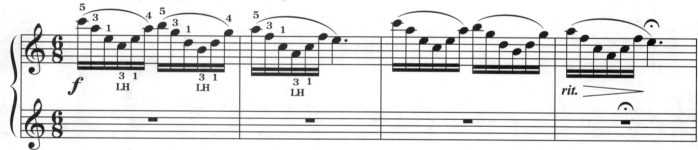

With energy (♩. = 58)
Both hands one octave higher throughout

Middle

Low

High

Middle

Low

High

Middle

Low

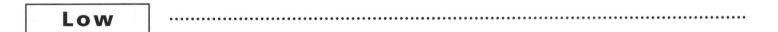

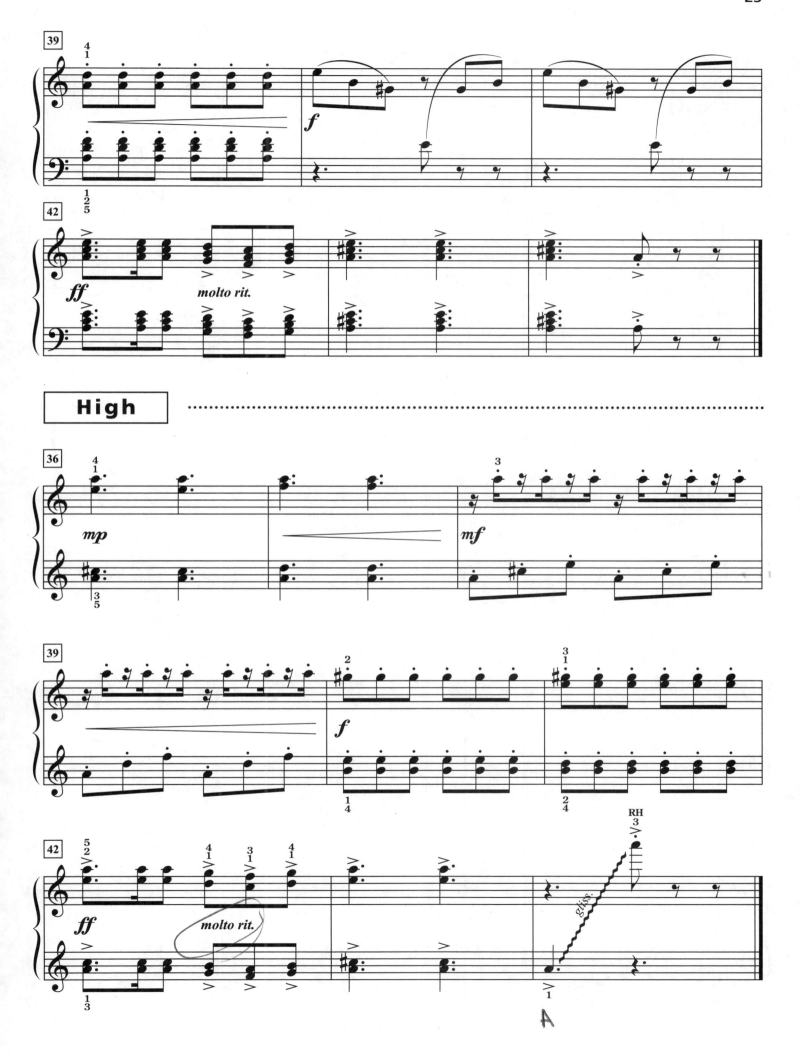

High

Riverbend Rag

Melody Bober

Middle

Low

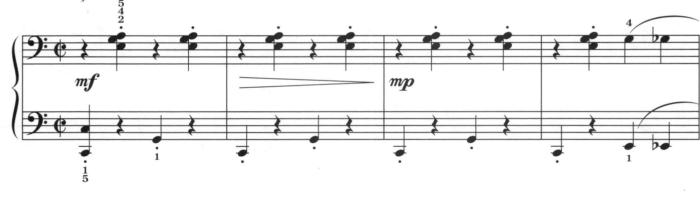

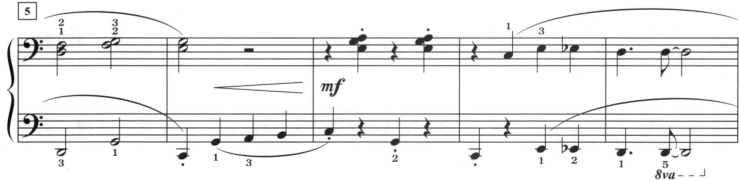

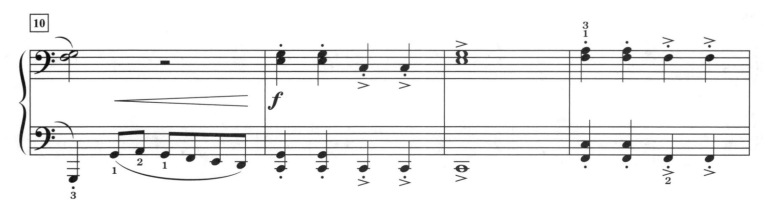

High

Both hands one octave higher throughout

Cheerfully (♩ = 72)

Middle

Low

Middle

Low

High

Middle

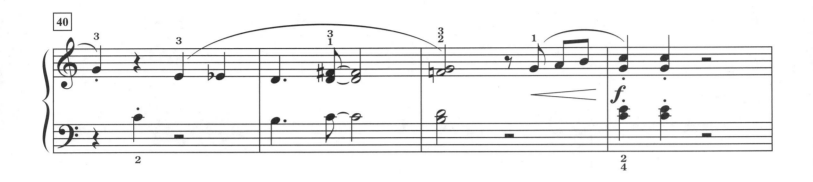

Low